The Ultimate Football Quiz

LAGOON
BOOKS

Series Editor: Heather Dickson
Research: David Lever and Anneli Harrison
Additional contributors: Sheila Harding,
Ann Marangos, Peter Kirkham
Photographs: Sportsphoto Ltd
Page design and layout: Linley Clode
Cover design: Gary Inwood Studios

Published by:
LAGOON BOOKS
PO BOX 311, KT2 5QW, UK

ISBN: 1899712747

© LAGOON BOOKS, 1999
Lagoon Books is a trade mark of
Lagoon Trading Company Limited.
All rights reserved.

Printed in Singapore

The Ultimate
Football Quiz

LAGOON
BOOKS

Introduction

Dribble and shoot your way through this fantastic football quiz.

Aimed at experts, amateurs and ignoramuses alike, it's an all-round winner with questions on everything from cup finals to national leagues. If you don't know who won the European Championship in 1992, then perhaps you know the capacity of Wembley Stadium? If you don't know which team has Hercules the Lion as a mascot, then perhaps you know in which district of Paris you'll find the Stade de France? What colour boots Ronaldo wore in France '98? Or who said: "We've signed five foreigners over the Summer. But I'll be on hand to learn them English"?

For similar questions and much, much more, read on....

....but if you're clued up and feeling competitive, why not tackle the ultimate football challenge and keep score as you read through the book?

SCORING: If the question has only one answer, score 8 points. If the question has eight separate answers, score 1 point for each answer you get correct. At the end of the book, add up your score and see how you fared.

> **Between 1 and 100**
> Partick Thistle have let you go!
>
> **Between 101 and 200**
> You've been dropped to the reserves
>
> **Between 201 and 300**
> You're mid table in the First Division
>
> **Between 301 and 400**
> You're Premiership front-runners
>
> **Between 401 and 544**
> Congratulations – you're in the World Cup!

To play the Ultimate Football Quiz, split players into two teams. Each team should nominate one player to read the questions. Team 1 should choose a page in the book and read the questions on that page to Team 2. Team 2 should then choose another page and read the questions on that page to Team 1. At the end of the game count how many points each team has scored – the team with the highest score is the winner!

Who...?

(A) Scored the first ever goal in the World Cup

(B) Was named English Footballer of the Year in 1997

(C) Threw his shirt at Michel Platini in France '98

(D) Were the champions in the Belgian League 1997/98

(E) Does the singer/songwriter Elvis Costello support

(F) Cost Manchester United £10.75 million to shore up their defence in 1998

(G) Was the West German goalkeeper in the 1966 World Cup Final

(H) Was the first ever person to play and coach in the World Cup Final

1

What are these players otherwise known as?

A The King Of The Hill

B Choccy

C El Magnifico

D The Genie

E Shaggy

F The Black Arrow

G Psycho

H Crazy Horse

2

They all got the boot. Which one and why?

(A) Paolo Rossi

(B) Grzegorz Lato

(C) Mario Kempes

(D) Gary Lineker

(E) Sandor Kocsis

(F) Gerd Muller

(G) Eusebio

(H) Just Fontaine

3

What are all
of these?

A Paget's "New Bing"

B W Shillcock's "McGregor"

C Sugg's "Improved Owl"

D Richard Daft's "County"

E Deverell Bros "Europa"

F "The Patent Buttonless"

G Mitre "Ultimax"

H Thompson's "T Panelling"

4

Rock 'n' Roll Footballers!
Who had a hit with...?

A   Oei Oei Oei

B   Moleque Danado

C   Ajax Is De Konig

D   Head over Heels in Love

E   Fog on the Tyne

F   Het is fijn in Italie Te Zijn

G   Diamond Lights

H   1-0 Fur Deine Liebe

5

Ronaldo, 1996

Where was the World Cup held in...?

A 1930

B 1934

C 1950

D 1954

E 1958

F 1962

G 1982

H 1942

Which British teams play at the following grounds?

A Gresty Road

B Highfield Road

C Maine Road

D Boothferry Park

E Vicarage Road

F Portman Road

G St. James's Park

H Easter Road

Who did they manage in France '98?

(A) Miroslav Blazevic

(B) Daniel Passarella

(C) Nelson Acosta

(D) Aime Jacquet

(E) Cesare Maldini

(F) Steve Sampson

(G) Bo Johansson

(H) Bum-Kun Cha

8

How much did...?

(A) Manchester United pay for striker Dwight Yorke in August 1998

(B) Peter Johnson pay for Everton in 1994

(C) It cost to make the original FA Cup in 1827

(D) Fulham player Johnny Haynes increase his weekly wage by in 1961

(E) Ken Bates pay for Chelsea

(F) Aston Villa pay for Stan Collymore

(G) Rotherham United pay out in their 1996/97 annual wage bill

(H) Terry Venables pay for Portsmouth

Where are these stadiums?

(A) Maracana Stadium

(B) Louis II Stadium

(C) Tynecastle Stadium

(D) San Siro Stadium

(E) Estadio de Luz

(F) Ashton Gate

(G) Stade de France

(H) Stadio Olimpico

10

Which...?

A Country won the European U18s Championship in 1998

B Team came third in France '98

C Three teams were relegated from the English Premiership in 1998

D Team did Arsenal beat in the 1998 FA Cup Final

E Hollywood superstar has a stadium named after him

F Team knocked Manchester United out of Europe in 1997

G Team did Chelsea beat to claim the European Cup Winner's Cup in 1998

H Team dyed their hair blond during France '98

11

What nationality are the following players?

A Elton John Borges

B Jim Bong-Soo

C Giovanni Van Bronckhorst

D Dan Eggen

E Airton Luis Oliveira Barroso

F Hugo Overlar

G Olaf Thon

H Jang Dae Il

12

Michael Owen, 1997

How many goals have these players scored for Newcastle United?

A Barrie Thomas (1962-64)

B Albert Shepherd (1908-14)

C Malcolm McDonald (1971-76)

D Mick Quinn (1989-93)

E Hughie Gallagher (1925-30)

F Jack Smith (1934-38)

G Jackie Milburn (1946-57)

H Andy Cole (1993-95)

13

Who wrote these books?

A *They Used To Play On Grass*

B *United!*

C *Harry's Game*

D *Odd Man Out*

E *A Will To Win*

F *My Story So Far*

G *Don't Call Me Happy*

H *White Lines*

What...?

A Is so special about Vitesse Arnhem's stadium

B Did Constant Vanden Stock of Anderlecht FC admit to in 1984

C Did Croatian coach, Miroslav Blazevic wear during France '98

D Is Dennis Bergkamp's biggest fear

E Was the name of the Argentinian who David Beckham kicked in France '98 to get sent off

F English team originally played under the name "St. Luke's Blakenhall"

G Is referee David Elleray's day job

H Country did Moustafa Kamel keep goal for in 1934

Who said...?

A "The Beatles were sitting a few rows in front, but I was more interested in Brian Clough"

B "I like to have a funny moment"

C "If Bergkamp thinks he is going to set the world alight, he can forget it..."

D "No football should be shown on television for three years"

E "I'm not doing this (buying a club) to raise my profile"

F "We've played here (at Wembley) a dozen times...that's more than Chelsea"

G "In international football, you have to be able to handle the ball"

H "Beckham has two feet, which a lot of people say players don't have now"

16

Where were these England players born?

A Luther Blissett

B Terry Butcher

C John Salako

D Rob Jones

E Cyrille Regis

F Tony Dorigo

G John Barnes

H Graeme Le Saux

17

What injury have all these players and ex-players suffered?

A Alan Shearer

B John Salako

C Steve Coppell

D Iain Durrant

E Paul Lake

F Ben Thornley

G Brian Clough

H Paul Gascoigne

18

Who did they manage in Euro '96?

(A) Anghel Lordanescu

(B) Arrigo Sacchi

(C) Guus Hiddink

(D) Bertie Vogts

(E) Arthur Jorge

(F) Dusan Uhrin

(G) Fatih Terim

(H) Javier Clemente

19

Diego Maradona, 1994

Who...?

A Refused to play in the 1950 World Cup

B Did the 1934 Italy World Cup side salute before the Final

C Captained Brazil to victory in the 1970 World Cup Final

D Wrote the 1998 World Cup theme song for Germany

E Beat Germany in the quarter-finals of the 1994 World Cup

F Founded one of Argentina's leading clubs Boca Juniors

G Refused to let his team switch shirts in a 1966 World Cup quarter-final

H Said "If Barnsley win tomorrow, we only need seven points from our last two games to pip them"

20

What is...?

A Futebol de salao

B The Magnus Effect

C The Little Tin Idol

D A golden goal

E The lofted pass

F UEFA

G The byline

H The German Football League called

Father and Son.
Spot the odd pair out

A Harry and Jamie Rednapp

B Frank and Frankie Lampard jnr

C Johan and Jordi Cruyff

D Les and Rio Ferdinand

E George and George Eastham

F Jean and Youri Djorkjaeff

G Florian and Florian Albert

H Kenny and Paul Dalglish

22

In which city will you find...?

A OFK, Partizan and Red Star

B Slavia, Sparta and Dukla

C Rapid, First and Wacker

D Levski, CSKA and Spartak

E Brondby

F Skonto, Amstrig and Kvadrats

G Steaua, Dinamo and Venus

H Go Ahead Eagles

Women's football

A Who won the Women's World Cup in Sweden in 1995?

B Who are "The Spitfires"?

C Who was the first English woman to play semi-professional football for Roma?

D When was the first official English Women's football match?

E Who was it between and who won?

F Who are "The Ironesses"?

G Who wrote: "I lost my heart to the Belles"?

H Which team topped the National Division in 1998?

How many...?

(A) Goals did Oleg Salenko score against Cameroon in the 1994 World Cup Finals

(B) Times did West Germany win the World Cup

(C) World Cup competitions including 1998 have England qualified for

(D) Internationals has Peter Shilton played

(E) Times have Brazil won the World Cup

(F) Goals did Brazil beat England by in Mexico '70

(G) Goals did Salvatore Schillaci score in Italy '90

(H) Did he score in the rest of his international career

25

Famous fans.
Who supports whom?

(A) Silvio Berlusconi

(B) Damien Hirst

(C) Cardinal Basil Hume

(D) Hunter Davies

(E) Jacques Chirac

(F) Tony Benn

(G) Melanie Chisholm (Sporty Spice)

(H) Ronnie Biggs

26

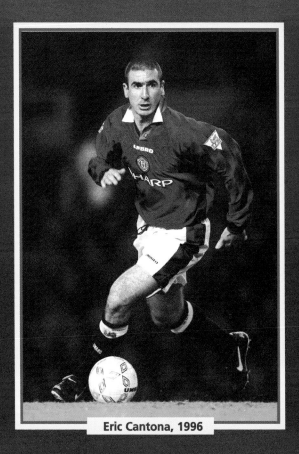

Eric Cantona, 1996

Which...?

A City kicked off the 1994 World Cup

B Italian player from the 1982 World Cup Final played in the 1998 UEFA Cup Final for Inter Milan

C Brazilian player scored a hat-trick despite playing barefoot in the 1938 World Cup against Poland

D Football team did heavyweight boxer Joe Louis sign for in 1944

E Shirt number did Eusebio and Gerd Muller wear

F Stadium is in Budapest – Ferencvaros or the Nou Camp stadium

G Leslie did Lee Chapman marry, Judd or Ash

H Barnsley player said the women of Barnsley were "far uglier" than those of his native country, Macedonia

27

Would you believe it!

A How old was Neil McBain when he played in goal for New Brighton in 1947?

B Ted Sagar joined Everton on 26 March 1929. How many years did he stay with the club?

C How many goals did Ted MacDougall score for Bournemouth in the FA Cup first round against Margate in 1971?

D What happened to Birmingham City goalkeeper Tony Coton in his debut in 1980?

E In which year did the first FA Cup Final replay take place

F Chesterfield changed their blue shirts for what in 1890?

G Why did Spurs almost lose their amateur status in 1893?

H What year did referees start using whistles?

What are these teams otherwise known as?

A The Addicks

B The Pirates

C The Minstermen

D The Merry Millers

E The Blades

F The Throstles

G The Potters

H The Irons

29

Firsts!

A What year was the first FA Cup Final played at Wembley?

B What year did Aston Villa become League Champions for the first time since 1910?

C Stanley Matthews became the first footballer to be knighted. When?

D What year was the first £200,000 transfer in Britain?

E What was the year of the first floodlit match in the Football League?

F What year was the Players' Union formed?

G What year did England enter the World Cup for the first time?

H What year was the first British International Championship?

Match the fanzines to the clubs

A *Come In Number 7*

B *The Red Card*

C *Rub of The Greens*

D *Sex and Chocolate Aren't As Good As Football*

E *Mad as a Hatter*

F *The Sheeping Giant*

G *The Zulu*

H *Follow the Yellow Brick Road*

31

What have all of the following done?

A Eklind

B Reader

C Filho

D Puhl

E Guigue

F Langenus

G Glockner

H Ling

32

Strange but true!

A How much did Chelsea's first ever goal-keeper, William "Fatty" Foulke's weigh?

B Argentinian team River Plate paid £15,000 for striker Gerado Castro. Why so little?

C Crystal Palace discovered Ian Wright playing for which side?

D What was England's World Cup song in 1966?

E Who is Andy Cole's favourite singer?

F Which film theme was played when Wimbledon took to the field in the 1997/98 season?

G Who said about whom, "He's an a******* not worth two bob, never mind two million!"?

H Who wrote the Albanian World Cup song in 1994?

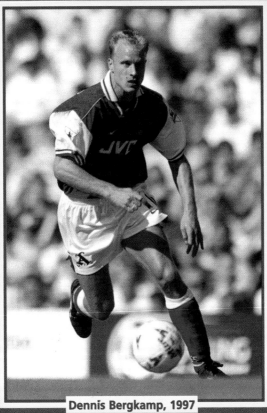

Dennis Bergkamp, 1997

The French venues of the 1998 World Cup

A What is the name of the stadium in Bordeaux?

B Nantes is home to which French team?

C What is the capacity of the stadium in Lyon?

D What is Saint Etienne's Geoffroy Guichard Stadium otherwise known as?

E Toulouse is famous for Concorde. Which famous footballer was also born there?

F The Montpellier Mosson Stadium is built on which avenue?

G Does Lens lie north or south of Paris?

H In which part of Paris is the Stade de France?

34

Name the manager who said...

(A) "You're not a real manager unless you've been sacked"

(B) "Some people think football is a matter of life and death...I can assure them it is much more serious than that"

(C) "Some teams are so negative they could be sponsored by Kodak"

(D) "There's no fun in football any more. We'll end up playing in cemeteries."

(E) "Women should be in the kitchen, the discotheque and the boutique, but not in football"

(F) "Everything about being a professional sportsman is about the winning"

(G) "The coach means a lot but it's the players who play"

(H) "There are more hooligans in the House of Commons than at a football match"

'Ere We Go, 'Ere We Go...
Put the player or team to the chant or song

A "He's blond, he's quick, his name's a porno flick..."

B "Daydream Believer"

C "The Wheelbarrow Song"

D "Blue Moon"

E "Blue is the Colour"

F "I'm Forever Blowing Bubbles"

G "You'll Never Walk Alone"

H "Toon Army"

In which countries will you find these teams?

(A) Ob

(B) If

(C) Irony Ashdod

(D) Kolkheti-1913 POTI

(E) Pas

(F) Army

(G) Floriana

(H) FC Dodo

The World Cup

A Which English player was wrongly arrested in 1970, suspected of theft?

B How many pounds of sausages did the England squad consume in Mexico '70?

C How many Argentinians were sent off in the 1990 World Cup Final?

D What was so special about the TV transmission in England of Mexico '70?

E How many teams competed in France '98?

F Who was the first player to miss a penalty in the World Cup?

G Scotland were unbeaten in the 1974 World Cup Finals. True or false?

H What had to be changed in the first minute of the England v West Germany game in 1970?

Balls!

A What happened to the ball in the FA Cup Final in 1946?

B What happened to the ball in the FA Cup Final the next year?

C Which is heavier, the football of the 1940s or the modern-day football?

D What happened to the match ball with which Germany won the 1996 European Championships?

E Who said: "The trouble that day was that they used an orange ball...I was afraid to kick it."?

F Which female children's TV presenter is a Manchester United fan?

G What happened when Peter Knowles kicked the ball out of the stadium in 1960?

H According to legend, after the Romans had invaded Britain, they played football with what?

Who said... ?

A "I love English football...you play for 75 minutes each match, rather than 60 as they do in Italy."

B "I have never forgotten that I am black...I used to get people who didn't know...because I don't look black"

C "You'd have to be on drugs to spit at Vinnie. He ran into it"

D "If I've learned anything, I've learned not to sign any more Romanians"

E "We've signed five foreigners over the Summer. But I'll be on hand to learn them English"

F "I'm not star-struck around players... I'm the biggest star here"

G "Oh no, bloody hell. French? I've got to play for a Frenchman? You must be joking"

H "It wasn't diving. I got booked for saying their captain had a big nose"

40

Ruud Gullit, 1995

What do they all mean?

A Kac Kac (Turkish)

B Vad star de (Swedish)

C Como va el partido (Spanish)

D Kak schyot (Russian)

E Ci este scorul (Romanian)

F Como esta o jogo (Portuguese)

G Jaki jest wynik (Polish)

H Come siamo (Italian)

41

Who...?

A Is the most successful club in the Czech Republic

B Won the European Championships in 1992

C Are the "Lilywhites" better known as

D Are known as "The Soup Eaters" in Bulgaria

E Was England's first million-pound player

F Are the co-hosts of Euro 2000

G Introduced the 4-4-2 formation to the English game

H Other than Manchester United, are known as "The Red Devils"

42

What...?

A Year was the Heysel Stadium disaster

B Was the name of the Belgian player banned for life for nearly blinding another player in 1996

C Year was the red and yellow card system first introduced

D Are the "Kupa Na Balgariya" and the "Profi-Liga Kupa"

E Was the age of Zvonimir Boban when he became captain of Croatia

F Is Wembley's capacity

G Year did Wimbledon win the FA Cup

H Did BSKYB pay for the live TV football rights in 1992

43

Match the Mascots with their teams

A The Mighty Mariner

B Stamford the Lion

C Bluey the Shire Horse

D Samson and Delilah the Cats

E Hercules the Lion

F Nellie the Elephant

G Billy the Bantam

H The Baggie Bird

44

In which country were each of these Internationals born?

(A) Roberto Di Matteo (Italy)

(B) Wagner Lopes (Japan)

(C) Thomas Dooley (USA)

(D) Luis Oliveira (Belgium)

(E) Matt Elliott (Scotland)

(F) Preki Radosavljevic (USA)

(G) Romarin Billong (Cameroon)

(H) Robbie Earle (Jamaica)

Match these birds with their teams?

(A) The Bluebirds

(B) The Seagulls

(C) The Owls

(D) The Canaries

(E) The Robins

(F) The Eagles

(G) The Swans

(H) The Magpies

What did the Queen do to all of these players?

A Peter Shilton

B Joe Mercer

C Bobby Moore

D Tom Finney

E Bryan Robson

F George Eastham

G Emlyn Hughes

H Brian Clough

47

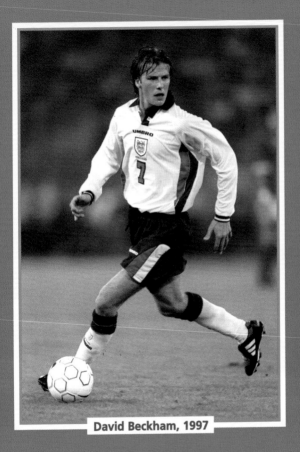

David Beckham, 1997

Which...?

A Football team in England have never played at home

B Club was nicknamed "The Old Reds"

C Club was known as "Riverside Albion"

D East German side was the footballing branch of the Stasi secret police

E Ground was used for a Hovis TV advert in the 1970s

F Gulf State did England play in the 1982 World Cup

G Manager took Norwich City to the top flight for the first time

H Club did Alf Ramsey take over after leaving England

Who said...?

A "You need 14 players performing well to win anything"

B "I can show Maradona a few tricks to get into shape"

C "I'd stop Gazza slapping women and I'd drink him... under the table"

D "I've got six bull terriers, a rottweiler and a bulldog"

E "One of the most pinnacle examples of what Jesus did was forgiveness"

F "(£7,000 a week) may be enough for the homeless, but not for an international striker"

G "I can see the carrot at the end of the tunnel"

H "Referee error is part of the joy of the game"

Match the team to the fanzine

A *4,000 holes*

B *Route One*

C *Deranged Ferret*

D *Monkey Business*

E *The Water in Majorca*

F *The Memoirs of Seth Bottomley*

G *No-One Likes Us*

H *It's Half Past Four and We're 2-0 Down*

The World Cup

A Wales and Northern Ireland both reached the quarter-finals in 1938. True or false?

B What was the average age of the 1950 English World Cup Finals team?

C How much was an English player's pocket money in Brazil during the 1950 World Cup?

D How many goals were scored in total in the World Cup Finals of 1938?

E There were no team doctors taken to Brazil for the 1950 World Cup Finals by the English team. True or false?

F What were allowed for the first time in Mexico '70?

G Did Scotland qualify for the 1950 World Cup?

H Who was the England team's cook in 1950?

51

Strange but true!

A What did Kuwait use as their lucky mascot in 1982?

B After how many games was Carlos Albert Parreira sacked as coach of Saudi Arabia in France '98?

C How did "Pickles", the World Cup trophy-finding dog, die?

D What did Mussolini's telegram to the Italian team competing in the 1938 World Cup say?

E How many miles did Pedro Gatica cycle to watch his team, Argentina, play in Mexico '86?

F What happened to him when he arrived in Mexico?

G What were substituted for the first time ever in 1994, Bulgaria v Mexico?

H What was Miguel Baron (Mexican coach in 1994) a graduate in?

52

The Boys from Brazil!

A Which Brazilian player from the World Cup squad '98 has an Olympic medal?

B Who is Rai's footballing brother?

C How much in US dollars, did Real Betis pay for Denilson?

D Who is known as ET?

E How many yards did Roberto Carlos' freekick travel in Le Tournoi against France?

F Who is Crizam Cesar de Oliveira?

G Who is Edson Arantes do Nascimento?

H Which player's name means "Dopey" in Portuguese?

53

Which giants did they slay in the English FA Cup?

A Bournemouth (1984)

B Boston United (1975)

C Hereford United (1972)

D Yeovil (1949)

E Wrexham (1992)

F Sutton United (1989)

G Colchester United (1971)

H Worcester City (1959)

54

Paul Gascoigne, 1998

Which African teams are known by the following nicknames?

A Bafana Bafana

B Indomitable Lions

C Desert Warriors

D Stallions

E Leopards

F Azingo Nationale

G Black Stars

H Elephants

55

Match the following boot names to the correct brands

A Integrity

B Mercurial

C Zico Brazil

D Executive

E Tacto

F Velocita

G King

H Copa

What do these ex-players have in common?

(A) Jim Standen

(B) Arnie Sidebottom

(C) Laurie Fishlock

(D) Willie Watson

(E) Chris Balderstone

(F) Brian Close

(G) Ken Taylor

(H) Arthur Milton

57

What in God's name do they do? And for which clubs?

(A) Simon Stevenette

(B) Mervyn Terrett

(C) Peter Amos

(D) Elwin Cockett

(E) Robert de Berry

(F) Mark Kichenside

(G) Brian Rice

(H) Richard Chewter

58

Football and the silver screen

A Who played the footballing coach in the film *Kes*?

B Which team did Sean Bean play for in the film, *When Saturday Comes*?

C Which two footballers acted in *Boys From The Black Stuff*?

D Name Eric Cantona's regal movie of 1998?

E Which film did the Scotland team watch before their Euro '96 matches?

F Whose legs were used to represent the lead character's on the pitch in *All In the Game*?

G Which two ex-players appeared in *The Perfect Match*?

H Who plays the hard man in *Lock, Stock and Two Smoking Barrels*?

50

Would you believe it!

(A) How many goals did Ronald and Frank de Boer score in their debut game for De Zoaven?

(B) Which two players scored on their debuts for Tottenham Hotspur and Sheffield Wednesday, in the same match?

(C) How old was Albert Geldard on his debut for Bradford Park Avenue?

(D) Why was Maradona's debut for Argentinos Juniors delayed?

(E) Why was Maradona's debut for Boca Juniors unusual?

(F) How old was David Donaldson in his debut game for Wimbledon in 1977?

(G) What did Roy Hollis do in his debut match for Norwich in 1948?

(H) What happened to Marcus Gayle in his debut match for the England youth team?

60

Who...?

A Were the Five Violins

B Were the first winners of the Super Cup, in 1971

C Experimented with a purple and pink strip, described as "a Summer pudding"

D Once described himself as "a wee fat number four"

E Were known as the "Quality Street Kids"

F Were the first club to carry a sponsor's name on their shirts

G Has the widest pitch in the Football League

H Were "The Diddy Men"

61

Jurgen Klinsmann, 1997

Which...?

A Midfielder was described as "10 stone of barbed wire"

B Player was known as "The Clown Prince of Soccer"

C Is the only ground in the UK to have a pub on every corner

D Goalkeeper takes freekicks for club and country

E European side are known as "The Policemen"

F Two teams play their home matches at Selhurst Park

G Scottish player was the first to be sold for £1 million

H English player was the first to be sent off during an International

62

How many...?

A Hat-tricks did Dixie Dean score in his career

B Registered footballers were there in China in 1995

C Steps between the boundary wall of Dundee's Dens Park and Dundee United's Tannadice

D Footballing sons did George Wilkins have

E Times did George Best get sent off during his career

F Years did Andrew Smailes remain at Rotherham United

G Languages does Arsene Wenger speak

H People watched Romania v Peru in the World Cup Finals in 1930

What do all these players have in common?

A Steve Howey

B Tommy Baldwin

C Mick Hazard

D Kevin Dillon

E Gavin Oliver

F Michael Wardrobe

G Steve Carter

H Lee Howey

64

What is the game?

A It was first played in 1947

B It was invented by Peter Adolph

C It was orginally made of cardboard, cellulose, wire and paper

D It was going to be called "Hobby hawk"

E Its current name is Latin for hawk

F It won a top award in 1988

G It is played by over 5 million people worldwide

H Oasis, Primal Scream and the Beastie Boys are big fans

What coloured boots did they wear in France '98?

A Taffarel (Brazil)

B Rigobert Song (Cameroon)

C Clarence Seedorf (Holland)

D Cuauhtemoc Bianco (Mexico)

E Alessandro Del Piero (Italy)

F Kjetil Redal (Norway)

G Said Chiba (Morocco)

H Ronaldo (Brazil)

Which...?

A League has a team called "Robin Hood"

B Country's first league championship was won by the British Police

C Scottish team play at Pittodrie

D Player was African Footballer of the Year in 1976 and 1990

E European manager has the same name as his country's favourite drink

F Is Eusebio's surname, Gomes or Ferreira

G South American footballer has been Footballer of the Year the most times

H Nation, other than Brazil, did Leonidas play for

How much do you know about Major League Soccer?

A In what year was the League set up?

B The League continued during the 1998 World Cup Finals. True or false?

C Who were the double winners in 1996?

D Which two clubs did Mexican goalkeeper Jorge Campos play for before returning to his native country?

E Which two English clubs did Major League Soccer star goalie Jurgen Sommer previously play for?

F Name the former Scottish international striker who captains the Kansas City Wizards?

G How many points do you get for a draw in Major League Soccer?

H Name the DC United manager

Alan Shearer, 1996

Solutions

Page 1
A) Lucien Laurent B) Dennis Bergkamp C) Hristo Stoichkov (Bulgaria) D) Club Bruges E) Liverpool F) Jaap Stam G) Hans Tilkowski H) Mario Zagalo (1958 player, 1970 coach)

Page 2
A) Theodore Whitmore B) Brian McClair C) David Ginola D) Zoubeir Beya (Tunisia) E) Steve McManaman and Darren Anderton F) Faustino Asprilla G) Stuart Pearce H) Emlyn Hughes

Page 3
The Golden Boot for being top scorer in the World Cup Finals

Page 4
They are all footballs

Page 5
A) Johan Cruyff B) Pele C) Gerrie and Arnold Muhren D) Kevin Keegan E) Paul Gascoigne and Lindisfarne F) Marco Van Basten and Frank Rijkaard G) Glenn Hoddle and Chris Waddle H) Franz Beckenbauer

Page 6
A) Uruguay B) Italy C) Brazil D) Switzerland E) Sweden F) Chile G) Spain H) There wasn't one because of the Second World War

Page 7
A) Crewe Alexandra B) Coventry City

Solutions

C) Manchester City D) Hull City E) Watford
F) Ipswich Town G) Newcastle United and
Exeter City H) Hibernian

Page 8
A) Croatia B) Argentina C) Chile D) France E) Italy
F) USA G) Denmark H) South Korea

Page 9
A) £12.6 million B) £10 million C) £20 D) £80 E) £1
F) £7.5 million G) £1,106,000 H) £1

Page 10
A) Rio de Janeiro, Brazil B) Monaco C) Edinburgh,
Scotland D) Milan, Italy E) Lisbon, Portugal
F) Bristol, England G) Paris, France H) Rome, Italy

Page 11
A) Republic of Ireland B) Croatia C) Crystal Palace,
Bolton, Barnsley D) Newcastle United
E) Arnold Schwarzenegger (Austria's Sturm
Graz play there) F) AS Monaco G) VFB Stuttgart
H) Romania

Page 12
A) Brazilian B) South Korean C) Dutch D)
Norwegian E) Belgian F) Paraguan G) German
H) South Korean

Page 13
A) 50 B) 92 C) 121 D) 63 E) 143 F) 73
G) 200 H) 68

Solutions

Page 14

   A) Terry Venables **B)** Karren Brady **C)** Dave Bassett
   D) Brian McClair **E)** Alex Ferguson **F)** Alan Shearer
   G) John Hendrie **H)** Mel Stein

Page 15

   A) It has a retractable pitch and roof **B)** Paying a
referee 1 million Belgian Francs after a UEFA Cup
semi-final against Nottingham Forest **C)** A French
policeman's "kepi" **D)** Flying **E)** Diego Simeone
   F) Wolverhampton Wanderers **G)** Housemaster at
Harrow School **H)** Egypt

Page 16

   A) Delia Smith **B)** Paolo di Canio **C)** Alan Sugar
   D) Brian Clough **E)** Mohammed Al Fayad after his
takeover of Fulham **F)** Mick Jagger gigging at
Wembley **G)** Glenn Hoddle **H)** Jimmy Hill

Page 17

   A) Jamaica **B)** Singapore **C)** Nigeria
   D) Wales **E)** French Guyana **F)** Australia
   G) Jamaica **H)** Jersey

Page 18

   They have all suffered a cruciate ligament injury

Page 19

   A) Romania **B)** Italy **C)** Holland **D)** Germany
   E) Switzerland **F)** Czech Republic **G)** Turkey
   H) Spain

Solutions

Page 20
  A) Argentina **B)** Mussolini **C)** Carlos Alberto
  D) Mike Batt of "The Wombles" fame **E)** Bulgaria
  F) Patrick MacCarthy **G)** Sir Alf Ramsey
  H) Mark McGhee

Page 21
  A) A Brazilian 5-a-side football game **B)** The force
that causes a ball to swerve in flight **C)** A nickname
for the original FA Cup **D)** After a draw at full-
time, play continues until one team scores a
"Golden Goal", or for half an hour, when play is
stopped. If no one scores penalties are required.
  E) Giving sufficient lift to ball without excessive
power **F)** The Union of European Football
  G) The line between the corner flag and the goal
posts **H)** Bundesliga

Page 22
  Les and Rio are cousins, not father and son

Page 23
  A) Belgrade, Yugoslavia **B)** Prague,
Czech Republic **C)** Vienna, Austria **D)** Sofia,
Bulgaria **E)** Copenhagan, Denmark **F)** Riga, Latvia
  G) Bucharest, Romania **H)** Deventer, Holland

Page 24
  A) Norway **B)** Swindon Spitfires LFC
  C) Sue Lopez **D)** 1972 **E)** It was between Scotland
and England, England won 3-2 **F)** Scunthorpe

Solutions

Ladies **G)** Pete Davies **H)** Everton

Page 25
A) Five **B)** Three **C)** Ten **D)** 125 **E)** Four **F)** One
G) Six **H)** One

Page 26
A) AC Milan **B)** Leeds United **C)** Newcastle United
D) Spurs **E)** Paris St Germain **F)** Chesterfield
G) Liverpool **H)** Arsenal

Page 27
A) Chicago, USA **B)** Giuseppe Bergomi **C)** Leonidas
D) Liverpool **E)** 13 **F)** Ferencvaros Stadium **G)** Ash
H) Georgi Hristov

Page 28
A) 52 years and 4 months old **B)** 24 years
C) Nine **D)** He saved a penalty 85 seconds into
the match **E)** 1970 – between Chelsea and Leeds
United **F)** Union Jack shirts **G)** They were
accused of professionalism for buying a player
a pair of football boots **H)** 1878

Page 29
A) Charlton Athletic **B)** Bristol Rovers
C) York City **D)** Rotherham United **E)** Sheffield
United **F)** West Bromwich Albion **G)** Stoke City
H) Scunthorpe United

Solutions

Page 30
A) 1923 B) 1981 C) 1965 D) 1970 (Martin Peters, West Ham United to Spurs) E) 1956 (Portsmouth v Newcastle United) F) 1898 G) 1950 H) 1883

Page 31
A) Bristol City B) Chelsea C) Plymouth Argyle
D) Sunderland E) Luton Town F) Wrexham
G) Birmingham City H) Mansfield Town

Page 32
They have all refereed a World Cup Final

Page 33
A) 22 stone B) He was nine years old C) Dulwich Hamlet D) The World Cup Willie song E) Barrie White F) Mission Impossible G) Vinnie Jones on Gary Lineker H) Alexei Sayle

Page 34
A) Parc Lescure B) FC Nantes Atlantique C) 44,000
D) The Green Cauldron E) Just Fontaine F) Albert Einstein Avenue G) North H) Saint Denis

Page 35
A) Malcolm Allison B) Bill Shankly C) Tommy Docherty D) Terry Venables E) Ron Atkinson
F) Graeme Souness G) Kevin Keegan H) Brian Clough

Page 36
A) Emmanuel Petit B) Peter Reid C) Nottingham

Solutions

County **D)** Manchester City **E)** Chelsea **F)** West Ham United **G)** Liverpool **H)** Newcastle United

Page 37
A) Denmark **B)** Faroe Islands **C)** Israel **D)** Georgia **E)** Iran **F)** China **G)** Malta **H)** Mauritius

Page 38
A) Bobby Moore **B)** 400lb **C)** Two **D)** It was the first World Cup to be shown in colour **E)** 32 **F)** Cabrini (Italy) in Spain 1982 **G)** True, but they still failed to qualify for the knockout stages **H)** The ball

Page 39
A) It burst **B)** It burst again **C)** They are both the same weight **D)** It was kicked into the crowd by a jubilant German player and taken home by an England supporter **E)** Scottish defender Bobby Shearer after England's 9-3 victory over Scotland **F)** Zoe Ball **G)** He was charged 7s10d for a replacement **H)** The skulls of Britons they had slaughtered

Page 40
A) Gianluca Vialli **B)** Ryan Giggs **C)** Darren Anderton **D)** Harry Redknapp **E)** Dennis Wise **F)** Ken Bates **G)** Tony Adams **H)** Robert Lee (booked against Georgia)

Solutions

Page 41
  "What's the score?"

Page 42
  A) Sparta Prague B) Denmark C) Tottenham
  Hotspur and Preston North End D) CSKA Sofia
  E) Trevor Francis (from Birmingham City to
  Nottingham Forest) F) Belgium and Holland
  G) Sir Alf Ramsey H) The Belgian national team

Page 43
  A) 1985 B) Giles de Bilde C) 1970
  D) Bulgarian Cup competitions E) 18 F) 80,000
  G) 1988 H) £300 million

Page 44
  A) Grimsby Town B) Chelsea C) Ipswich Town
  D) Sunderland E) Aston Villa F) Leeds United
  G) Bradford City H) West Bromwich Albion

Page 45
  A) Switzerland B) Brazil C) Germany D) Brazil
  E) England F) Yugoslavia G) Chad H) England

Page 46
  A) Cardiff City B) Brighton and Hove Albion
  C) Sheffield Wednesday D) Norwich City E) Bristol
  City, Swindon Town and Wrexham F) Crystal Palace
  G) Swansea City H) Newcastle United or
  Nottingham County

Solutions

Page 47

She presented them all with the OBE

Page 48

A) Grimsby, their ground is in Cleethorpes
B) Accrington Stanley C) Cardiff City D) Dynamo Berlin E) Ewood Park, Blackburn F) Kuwait
G) Ron Saunders H) Birmingham City

Page 49

A) Steve Coppell B) Ben Johnson C) Ladies' Welterweight boxing champion Jane Couch
D) Julian Dicks E) Glenn Hoddle F) Pierre Van Hooijdonk, turning down Celtic's contract offer
G) Stuart Pearce H) David Elleray

Page 50

A) Blackburn Rovers B) Wimbledon C) Lincoln City
D) Hartlepool United E) West Ham United
F) Port Vale G) Millwall H) Dundee

Page 51

A) True B) 28 years C) £2 per day D) 84 E) True
F) Substitutes G) Yes, but they decided not to travel to Brazil H) Their manager Walter Winterbottom

Page 52

A) A live camel B) Two C) He was strangled by his own lead while chasing a cat in 1967 D) "Win or die" E) 820 miles F) He found he couldn't afford a ticket and his bike was stolen G) Goalposts
H) Dentistry

Solutions

Page 53

A) Aldair (Bronze medal in football, Atlanta 1996)
B) Socrates **C)** US$27 million **D)** Ronaldo
E) 40 yards **F)** Zinho **G)** Pele **H)** Dunga

Page 54

A) Bournemouth 2 Manchester United 0 (3rd round)
B) Derby County 1 Boston United 6 (3rd round)
C) Hereford United 2 Newcastle United 1 (3rd round replay) **D)** Yeovil Town 2 Sunderland 1 (4th round)
E) Wrexham 2 Arsenal 1 (3rd round)
F) Sutton United 2 Coventry City 1 (3rd round)
G) Colchester United 3 Leeds United 2 (5th round)
H) Worcester City 2 Liverpool 1 (3rd round)

Page 55

A) South Africa **B)** Cameroon **C)** Algeria
D) Burkina Faso **E)** Zaire **F)** Gabon **G)** Ghana
H) Ivory Coast

Page 56

A) Reebok **B)** Nike **C)** Diadora **D)** Asics **E)** Lotto
F) Umbro **G)** Puma **H)** Adidas

Page 57

They all played county cricket and professional
League Football

Page 58

They are all reverends, and were or are chaplains
to these teams **A)** Bristol Rovers **B)** Luton Town
C) Barnsley **D)** West Ham United **E)** Queen's Park

Solutions

Rangers **F)** Charlton Athletic **G)** Hartlepool United
H) Exeter City

Page 59

A) Brian Glover **B)** Sheffield United **C)** Sammy Lee
and Graeme Souness **D)** Elizabeth **E)** *Braveheart*
F) Michael Laudrup **G)** Denis Law and Bob Wilson
H) Vinnie Jones

Page 60

A) 5-a-piece. They were seven years old **B)** Jurgen
Klinsmann and Dan Petrescu **C)** 15 years and 158
days **D)** He was suspended for verbally abusing
players on the bench **E)** He played the first half for
Argentinos Juniors and the second half for Boca
Juniors **F)** 35 **G)** He scored a hat-trick against
Queen's Park Rangers in the first 20 minutes of
the game **H)** He broke his leg

Page 61

A) The Sporting Lisbon forwards of the 1950s and
1960s **B)** Ajax **C)** Aston Villa **D)** Kenny Dalglish
E) Celtic's 1960s Youngsters **F)** Kettering Town
G) Leyton Orient (80 yards) **H)** North Korea's 1966
World Cup team

Page 62

A) Billy Bremner **B)** Len Shackleton **C)** Griffin Park
(Brentford) **D)** Jose Luis Chilavert of Paraguay
E) Dynamo Moscow **F)** Wimbledon and Crystal
Palace **G)** Ian Ferguson **H)** Alan Mullery

Solutions

Page 63

A) 37 B) 2,253,000 C) 89 D) 4 (Ray, Dean, Graham and Steve E) Seven F) 29 years (He was a player, a trainer and manager) G) Six (French, English, German, Spanish, Italian and Japanese H) 300

Page 64

They all went to the same school
(St Aiden's, Sunderland)

Page 65

Subbuteo

Page 66

A) Green B) One red, one yellow C) Orange
D) Red and green halves E) Black and white stripes
F) Yellow G) Red H) Silver

Page 67

A) Surinam B) Israel's C) Aberdeen D) Roger Milla
E) Dick Advocaat F) Ferreira G) Diego Maradona
H) Uruguay

Page 68

A) 1996 B) True C) DC United D) Los Angeles Galaxy and Chicago Fire E) Luton Town and Queen's Park Rangers F) Mo Johnston
G) None – there are no draws in the Major League. If a match is tied, a shoot-out takes place to determine a winner H) Bruce Arena

Other titles available from Lagoon Books:

Where in the World Am I?
ISBN 1899712410

Pub Trivia Quiz
ISBN 189971250X

Who in the World Am 1?
ISBN 1899712275

Pocket Personality Quiz
ISBN 1899712909

Sports Trivia Quiz
ISBN 1899712267

Sporting Record-Breakers
ISBN 1899712755

The Ultimate Golf Quiz
ISBN 1899712739

All books can be ordered from bookshops by
quoting the above ISBN numbers.